Choosing a Puppy

Story by Jenny Giles
Illustrations by Sarah Davis

"Hello, Rachel! Hello, Sam!"
said Andy.
"Come and see the puppies.
They are here in the basket
with the mother dog."

Rachel said,

"Oh, look, Sam!

The puppies are asleep."

Dad said,

"Can you see a puppy you like?"

5

"I like this little brown puppy,"
said Rachel.

"I like this little puppy
with the **spots**," said Sam.

"The puppy with the spots

is awake," said Dad.

"Here he comes. Look, Sam!"

The puppy went
for a little walk.
"Come on, puppy,"
said Sam.

The puppy sat down.

He looked up at Rachel.

"Oh, look!" said Rachel.

"He **likes** me!

Come on, come to me . . . Spot!"

Spot got up,

and he went

to Sam and Rachel.

"We like **Spot**," said Sam.

"Can he come home with us?"

"Yes, he can go home with you today," said Andy.

"Oh, thank you, Andy," said Rachel.

"Come on, Spot," said Sam.

"You are coming home

with us."